RAILFREIGHT IN COLOUR

For the Modeller and Historian

David Cable

Ian Allan PUBLISHING

CONTENTS

Title page:
An overall view of a freight yard, this being Dover Town, where traffic from the train ferries was marshalled. The view shows three RFS Class 20s, two Class 08s and three Class 33s, plus a good assortment of wagons. Ships are entering and leaving the harbour.

Above:
Only one ARC 59 received the modified paint scheme before Hanson took over, namely No 59101 *Village of Whatley*. It is seen here at Shottesbrooke with the Merehead to Acton jumbo stone train, showing the silver band, yellow cab sides and small ARC logo that replaced the old grey and yellow. Taken in March 1999.

First published 2009

ISBN 978 0 7110 3364 1

Published by Ian Allan Publishing

an imprint of Ian Allan Publishing Ltd,
Hersham Surrey, KT12 4RG
Printed by Ian Allan Printing Ltd,
Hersham Surrey, KT12 4RG

Code: 0902/C

Visit the Ian Allan Publishing website at
www.ianallanpublishing.com

INTRODUCTION

This book covers the period from when the freight and departmental operations of British Rail became separate entities, up to and just including the privatisation of the railways. During these years, these activities became easily identifiable as a result of having their own colour schemes. This book is designed to be a reference title for both the historian and the model maker. It considers the rationale behind restructuring the railways and the formation of Railfreight, the services run with some information about the types of wagons used, but the greater part of the book deals with the locomotives and liveries. It also illustrates with photographs how freight operations have changed over the years, and highlights some of the traffic flows that have changed. These have been due both to negative and positive influences.

The negative effects have been mainly due to the bias of successive governments and the Treasury in favour of road over rail, leading to short-sighted decisions to abandon many sidings, with the virtual elimination of wagonload traffic, as well as the investment by industry in schemes such as oil pipelines, and the failure of the Channel Tunnel to develop business above the previous train-ferry levels. Other negative effects include the takeover of some major British industries by foreign companies leading to subsequent works closures such as steelworks, the reduction by successive governments in expenditure on major building projects such as new motorways, hospitals, prisons, etc, and last, but not least, the effects of the miners' strikes in the 1980s, leading to decisions to avoid coal for power stations in favour of piped natural gas.

However, on a positive note, there has been a large increase in the handling of containers, and the developments in motive power and rolling stock have led to a more reliable service to the customer.

Furthermore, changes as a result of Railfreight being more focused on its relations with customers, and the promotion of its own image, not only with the liveries of its locomotives, but also in signage of facilities, documentation-heading and various promotional items, have resulted in a more identifiable image for freight operations, especially since privatisation.

ACKNOWLEDGEMENTS

In writing this book, I would like to thank my good friend Brian Denton whose inside knowledge of freight workings as a driver at Eastleigh and as an ASLEF representative for many years, has enabled him to check various statements I have made. Colin Marsden, a fount of all knowledge, was of great value for putting me in touch with his website relating to locomotive names and depot mascots. The help given me by Mike Denny of Roundel Ltd in tracking down some obscure sector colours on locomotives, and his inside knowledge of the sector decal colour schemes, is also appreciated. The information provided since the mid 1990s by Freightmaster regarding scheduled freight services has been and still is invaluable.

Lastly, and in particular, I wish to thank Peter Waller and his colleagues at Ian Allan Publishing for their support and advice, and not least because they have actually paid me for doing this work!

David Cable
Hartley Wintney, Hants
2008

PHOTOGRAPHS

The publication shows motive power in all the different liveries and colour variations, the classes of locomotives allocated to freight and departmental duties, and many of the different types of train handled. The photographs were all taken by myself, and concentrate on both action and close-ups of locomotives, especially for the modellers, with some detail shots also included.

Photos were taken when opportunities arose, so purists may not be enamoured with those shots not taken in bright sunshine with the sun on the nose of the engine. Photos were taken either in the public domain or with the approval of nearby railway staff. A few of the photos have been used by my old friend Ron White of Colour Rail, but apart from one other, the rest have remained unpublished up to now.

Some post-privatisation pictures are included to show locomotives in old liveries and to give a variety of locations and train workings. A good many passenger workings have been handled by freight and departmental locomotives for various reasons, and non-freight sector engines have worked freight and departmental trains, but photos of such workings have been kept to a minimum.

The locations, some of which will be familiar, others less so and a few unique, cover much of Great Britain, having been visited in many cases as a result of my work with Blue Circle Industries (now Lafarge), and as a management consultant. This work took me to many places which enabled me to take photographs outside working hours during the lighter mornings and evenings. There is also a good selection based on my home area in the South of England. Some locations feature several times, but are used because they best illustrate a particular subject. There are parts of the country that I did not visit during these years, or when all locomotives were still in BR blue, and the reader must accept my apologies for such omissions and repetitions.

The photos are shown in the following sequence:

BR blue
Railfreight and Railfreight Red Stripe
Two-tone grey with sector decals
Trainload Freight – Loadhaul, Mainline, Transrail
Freightliner
Departmental grey and 'Dutch' livery
Private Companies – Yeoman, ARC, National Power, DRS
Non-standard Liveried Freight locomotives
Freight working by non-freight sector locomotives
EWS examples
Detail and miscellaneous photos

SECTORISATION

Up to around 1983, the finances of British Rail had largely been operated as one large corporate accounting system. But the Treasury, under the Thatcher government, started demanding more and more justification for the subsidy being made to a nationalised industry, not helped by the perennially road-prejudiced Department of Transport regarding the railway as a poor relation.

It had been realised that the increase of transport of freight by road in favour of rail since before World War 2 had resulted in the rail operations becoming substantial loss-makers, to the extent that by the early 1980s, the low level of business (road-to-rail ratio 8:1) was causing British Rail to endeavour to dispose of this class of activity.

So in 1983, the then Chairman of British Rail, Robert (later Sir Robert) Reid, introduced separate cost-centre accounting in order to assess the relative expenses incurred by each major activity, and thus to introduce accountability for

Below:
A skinhead '31' in original Railfreight grey and yellow is shunting empty coaching stock at Whitlingham Junction. No 31102 was noted in June 1987. High-intensity headlamp now fitted as standard.

each of these for the first time. Under this regime, the centres comprised Inter City, London and South East (later Network South East), Provincial (later Regional) Railways, Parcels, Departmental and Railfreight sectors, each of which was identified by separate colour schemes. In the main, this system showed that Inter City was more or less self-sufficient in terms of income and cost, but that the worst performers requiring subsidy were Provincial Railways and the Freight sector. Whilst it was possible to relate the costs within Provincial Railways to particular lines and services, this was not the case with Railfreight, which operated across the whole network.

In 1986, Foster Yeoman, which supplied aggregates from Merehead to the London and South East areas, had become so dissatisfied with the performance of around 60% efficiency offered by BR and Railfreight that it decided to undertake its own operations with its own locomotives and wagons, thus acting independently of Railfreight. The success of this private operation and its locomotives (Class 59) exceeding 95% efficiency was such that the ARC company operating from Whatley followed suit, and subsequently National Power based at Ferrybridge did likewise.

However, in 1987, with continuing

pressure from the Treasury, the new Chairman of BR, Sir Bob Reid, was forced to establish separate sub-sectors within the overall Railfreight sector, which was operating on a regional basis, to try to relate charges to customers to the costs and subsidy required. These sectors therefore became the equivalent of profit centres, and comprised the manufacturing entities of Coal, Construction, Metals and Petroleum, plus Distribution, and a little-used General sector. Container traffic was initially covered by the Distribution sector, but was sold off to the Freightliner company in 1995. Additionally, a sector was established for the handling of freight traffic through the Channel Tunnel, although it was first hoped that the locomotives involved (Class 92) would handle both freight and international overnight sleeper trains, which in the latter case never materialised. In 1989, many weed-killing services were handed over to Hunslet Barclay, who operated these trains with top-and-tailed Class 20s in their own livery.

Due to the profit-centre type structure and the management of these, it was inevitable that when resources of one sector were unavailable for various reasons, and recourse had to be taken to borrow another sector's equipment,

cross-accounting appeared on the scene, with all the associated complications and arguments (a precursor of today's financial cross-charging nightmare under privatisation!). This situation worsened in cases where a single train conveyed more than one sub-sector's load, leading to the sub-sectors preferring to operate trains entirely for their own loads, which led to some very uneconomic workings, for example one-wagon trains.

But, even though there had been some improvement in the level of goods handled by rail, the road sector had increased its business even more, to the extent that the ratio between them had increased in terms of ton miles to more than 11:1.

In 1994 the decision was made, in the lead-up to privatisation, to disband the sub-sectors and establish freight operations purely on a regional profit-centre basis, hoping to minimise cross-charging since most of the traffic flows were worked within each particular region, and where boundaries were crossed, the split of costs and profits could be determined in advance for all regular flows.

Three sectors, under the group title Trainload Freight, were operated – Mainline, covering the South East of England and the East Midlands; Loadhaul, covering the North and

East of England; and Transrail, covering Scotland, Wales and the North and West of England.

Freightliner and the Channel Tunnel operations remained independent of this structure. Departmental activities were absorbed into the appropriate region. A separate activity was established in 1995 to undertake the movement of nuclear flasks, operated by the Direct Rail Services (DRS) Company.

This system remained in situ until 1996 when the government privatised British Rail, and the old Trainload Freight sector became English, Welsh and Scottish Railways. Subsequent to this, certain traditional services were taken over by Freightliner, DRS and GB Railways, but these are outside the ambit of this publication.

FREIGHT AND DEPARTMENTAL TRAFFIC PATTERNS

Throughout the period covered by this book, freight and departmental services would have been seen at appropriate times at over 85% of the BR network in Great Britain.

Initially, much of the traffic was of a wagonload type, serving many locations – the Speedlink trains. These resulted in poor utilisation of assets and low return on investment. However, throughout this period, private industry invested more

and more in specialist wagons to enable bulk block loads to handle their traffic, which was a more cost-effective solution. Coal, cement, steel products and oil were, of course, handled in this manner from the 1960s.

Generally speaking, these services were kept clear as far as possible from main passenger operations and commuter peak services, although in the coal mining areas, there were many freight-only lines that enabled freight trains to run throughout the 24 hours without restrictions. There were few long-distance trains, and nothing to compare with cross-continental services as seen in Europe, North America or Australia. In comparison, British freight trains were relatively short.

Manufacturing and distribution operations tended to ship goods in the late afternoon/evening for delivery by next morning, in order to minimise stockholding levels. The exceptions to this were the continuous operation industries, such as steel works, cement plants and chemical processes. These needed some weekend service where it was impossible to build up stocks for normal weekday usage. Maritime loads also required some weekend services, especially containers, with their often high product values, and the demurrage costs for shipping.

Most freight traffic through the Channel Tunnel, which mainly left the continent in the evenings, required overnight transit in the UK, including weekends, where, for example, traffic had emanated from Bari in southern Italy.

Departmental work took place to some small extent during the normal working week, but predominantly at nights and at weekends, especially due to the service provided for track maintenance and consequent track closures.

Other factors which have affected traffic patterns include weekend premium payments for staff and the willingness of freight staff to work many unsociable shift patterns.

FREIGHT TRAFFIC

In the years between sectorisation and privatisation, freight traffic levels remained relatively static, but significant changes took place within those levels.

Traditional wagonload traffic was already being phased out and replaced by more block trains running between specific terminal points. As a

consequence, there was a major reduction in marshalling yards and local sidings.

Specialist wagons for block trains, many of which comprised bogie wagons, were introduced replacing many older types of standard wagon, although two-axle wagons were still used up to the end of the period for handling coal, cement, locomotive fuel oil, bitumen, china clay, sand, grain, gypsum and fly ash, as well as departmental duties, for example.

In the first stage of sectorisation, all freight and departmental traffic was undertaken by the one freight sector. At the second stage, the types of freight handled could be identified and allocated to a specific sector as detailed below. When Trainload Freight was established, each area covered all types of traffic within its own area, apart from departmental work.

COAL SECTOR
Coal for power stations, steelworks and cement works, fly ash and nuclear flasks.

CONSTRUCTION SECTOR
Aggregates, self discharge trains, cement, lime, gypsum, refuse, and Channel Tunnel components.

METALS SECTOR
Iron ore, slab, semi-finished products, wire coil, scrap metal, alumina, and limestone.

PETROLEUM SECTOR
Oil, petroleum, chemicals, bitumen, LPG, aviation fuel, and locomotive depot fuel.

RAILFREIGHT DISTRIBUTION
Speedlink/Enterprise Services, Channel Tunnel traffic, Ministry of Defence traffic, china clay, automotive, grain, sand, timber, and other miscellaneous traffic, LT tube trains.

FREIGHTLINER
Containers.

Many of these services are shown in the illustrations.

LOCOMOTIVE CLASSES BY SECTOR

The major classes operated by the Railfreight businesses during the 1983 to 1996 period were as follows:

Classes 08 (built at BR workshops), 20 (English Electric), 26 (BRCW), 31 (Brush), 33 (BRCW), 37 (English Electric), 47 (Brush and BR workshops), 56 (BR workshops and Electroputere in Romania), 58 (BR Workshops), 59 (General Motors, USA), 73 (English Electric), 86 and 90 (both BR Workshops), and latterly Class 60 (Brush) and 92 (Brush).

This section outlines the different classes allocated to each of the various freight sectors and colour schemes, recognising that there were many occasions when locomotives worked for

Below:
Not a normal coal sector duty, as No 37278 backs its MOD train from Ludgershall to Dinton off the branch onto the up main line at Andover in June 1992. No front number, no depot plate and no BR double arrow.

Above:
An ex-works RFD '90' with white wheel rims is taking a down Freightliner past Carpenders Park station in March 1993. No 90126 is named *Crewe Electric Depot*, but lacks a front number. Only a half-height RFD repeater strip is applied by the cab door.

different sectors and operations, even including passenger services. To a lesser extent, locomotives from non-freight sectors worked freight trains, and a selection of photographs are included to illustrate such events.

1. At the outset of sectorisation, all locomotives were in BR blue – indeed some stayed in blue throughout the whole period with which this book is concerned. A few classes mainly involved with freight work at the start of sectorisation, which were withdrawn/scrapped without carrying any Railfreight colour scheme, included 25, 40(97), 45(97), 46. Classes 81 and 85 also undertook many freight duties.

2. Locomotives which carried the first Railfreight livery including the Red Stripe variant were Classes 08 (a few), 20, 31, 37, 47, 56, 58.

3. Locomotives carrying the second Railfreight livery – the two-tone grey with decals – are grouped by sector. It should be realised that over time, individual locomotives were transferred between sectors and may have received more than one set of decals, and that some locomotives either lost or never received them.

Coal sector: 31, 37, 56, 58, 60
Construction sector: 31, 33, 37, 47, 56, 60
Metals sector: 37, 47, 56, 60
Petroleum sector: 31 (a few), 37, 47, 56 (1 only), 60
Railfreight Distribution (RFD): 08 (a few), 31 (1 only), 37, 47, 86/6, 87 (1 only), 90
RFD European sector: 47, 86/6, 90
European Passenger Services (EPS) sector: 92 (also 37 and 73 but not used for freight)
General sector: 31, 37, 47, 50, 60, 86 (see footnote)

4. Departmental liveried classes in both plain grey and 'Dutch' grey and yellow: 08/09, 31, 33, 37, 47, 50 (1 only), 56, 73. Some Class 37 engines in plain grey also carried a small sector decal.

5. Freightliner classes in grey with red triangles were: 47, 86/6, 90

6. Trainload Freight classes were allocated as follows, ignoring variations which are shown in photos:
    Mainline: 08/09 (a few), 37, 58, 60, 73
    Loadhaul: 37, 56, 60
    Transrail: 31 (a few), 37, 56, 60

7. Other private owners prior to privatisation:
    DRS: Class 20, later Class 37
    Hunslet Barclay: Class 20
    Yeoman, ARC, National Power: Class 59

Note regarding locomotives with General Sector decals:
Only around 20 locomotives carried this scheme, but three are of particular interest. Class 47 No 47145, which was painted in a rather garish blue colour, carried General Sector decals whilst on display at the Worksop open day as illustrated, but was later redecaled for RFD. Class 50 No 50149 carried these decals for many years before being repainted into Network South East colours, but was returned into General Sector livery after preservation for some time. Class 60 No 60010 was decaled for the 1991 RFD calendar, but was returned to normal Metals decals shortly afterwards. With the exception of 50149, all the other engines were changed quite quickly into the decal scheme appropriate for their type of business.

As a matter of interest, when the open day was held at Ripple Lane depot to introduce the Railfreight Sector decal scheme, a wooden mock-up of a Class 60 (which had not been commissioned at that time) was on display, embellished with General Sector decals.

LOCOMOTIVE COLOUR SCHEMES

The colour schemes used for locomotives for the three stages of Railfreight prior to privatisation were as follows:
STAGE 1.
The main body of the locomotive was painted in a light/medium grey from cantrail to the bottom of the bodyside. A medium size double arrow was applied in white. Cabs were painted in wrap-round yellow and roofs were black, with a standard orange electrification warning band applied at roof level.

All the equipment below the body, including the buffers, was black. The engine number was applied to the nearside cab front, and on the offside a red label with the word 'Railfreight' in white was stuck. These tended to become loose and be lost over time. Some locomotives were therefore fitted with cast plates with a red background in lieu. This feature was adopted for the whole of Class 58, many of which also had a similar plate across the cab ends below window level when a nameplate occupied the normal cab side location.

Two types of locomotive with narrow hoods and exposed chassis – Classes 20 and 58 – did not lend themselves to the basic design, and from the outset the edge of the chassis and buffer beam was painted in red. This brightened up the look of the locomotives to such an extent that it was adopted as standard, the band being painted along the bottom of the bodyside and buffer beam. A few engines even had red applied to the whole front end below the cab front.

Nameplates were fitted to the body in line with normal BR practice, except for the Class 58 which had nameplates on the offside cab side, and the few Class 20s which were named, where the nameplate was on the chassis at the end opposite to the cab.

As always there were exceptions with special variations, examples illustrated herein being No 20173 and No 47363.

Class 08 shunters often had individual depot treatment, including some painted in pre-nationalisation and even pre-grouping colours. These locomotives were not, of course, specifically allocated to freight duties.

A notable exception to being painted in Stage 1 colours was the Class 33. No electric locomotives were painted, and the Class 60 had not been introduced at that time.

Above:
A resplendent No 37023*Stratford* has been bulled up for display at Rickmansworth in May 1995. Worthy of special note are the blue headcode light surrounds, the blue front number, the Cockney Sparrow Depot Mascot plate, another Cockney Sparrow badge over the name plate, and the Quality Assured plate under the name. All in all, a credit to the lads at Stratford depot.

STAGE 2.

This stage introduced separate identification for each freight business sector, using individual decals for each. The basic scheme was two bands of grey, a medium colour band applied along the bodyside from the cantrail down to a level aligned with the bottom of the cab windows, with a light grey band down to the bottom of the bodyside below that, extending under the cab sides. Cab frames were painted black, and a half-height yellow front was applied. Roofs were black, and a standard orange electrification warning strip was put on at normal roof level. All equipment below bodyside level was painted black, as was the chassis of the Class 58.

Locomotive numbers were applied in black below the nearside cab windows with a BR double arrow logo beneath, either in white paint or in cast aluminium. A further number was applied on the yellow front end, comprising three figures, omitting the class. Depot mascot plates were fixed below the offside cab windows. Nameplates were attached as in Stage 1.

Sector decals were positioned one-third of the way along the bodyside from the front end, the sector identification part aligning at the top with the top of the light grey band. A repeater strip was positioned next to the offside cab door. An 'upper' square encompassed the top left corner of the decal, extending into the top grey band.

Coal sector: A yellow square with four black diamonds, with black 'upper' square. The repeater strip was yellow with black diamonds down it.

Construction sector: Blue and yellow square 'building' blocks with a blue 'upper' square. The repeater strip was alternate blue and yellow squares.

Metals sector: Blue and yellow 'V' shaped chevrons with a blue 'upper' square. The repeater was alternate blue and yellow chevrons.

Petroleum sector: Blue and yellow waves with a blue 'upper' square , with blue and yellow alternate waves for the repeater strip.

Railfreight Distribution: Two red diamonds on a yellow background, with a red 'upper' square. The repeater strip was formed of interlocking red and yellow triangles. For European services through the Channel Tunnel, a darker grey top band was used, and the roof was painted in dark blue. The words 'Railfreight Distribution' were applied to the lower bodyside.

Railfreight General: Alternate yellow and red rectangles forming a square with a red 'upper' square. The repeater strip comprised alternate red and yellow rectangles.

Freightliner: The standard two-tone grey scheme, with a red triangle and extra red 'hypotenuse' adjacent to the offside cab end.

European Passenger Services: The basic two-tone grey scheme was used with three silver rings of decreasing size applied by the nearside end cab (offside with Class 73). No repeater decals were used. Certain variations took place. The first two Class 37s painted in EPS livery had a much darker grey top band, subsequently repainted to standard grey. Two Class 92s carried small RFD decals and the words 'Railfreight Distribution' on the lower bodyside, and those owned by SNCF carried a small SNCF red flash under the nearside cab windows.

Departmental: A basic overall darkish grey scheme was initially introduced, with cab surrounds, doors and all equipment below bodyside level being black. Yellow cab fronts were as standard practice. Locomotive numbers, BR double arrows and cab mascots were applied as with the freight sector engines. This scheme was so drab that a decision was taken to apply a yellow band along the top of the bodyside from cantrail height to the level of the bottom of the cab windows.

As is always the case, there were various locomotives not adhering to standard practice. A few Class 37s in departmental grey carried very small metal decals on their bodysides, and even a batch of SNCF Class BB222xx locomotives, which were used for Channel Tunnel traffic prior to the introduction of the Class 92s, carried small RFD decals. Three Class 20s were restored to green livery with red framing, and other minor variations occurred. Particularly interesting were four Class 90s. No 90036 carried a 'prototype' RFD colour scheme with full orange ends and 'Railfreight Distribution' in red letters, and No 90028, No 90029 and No 90030 were painted in schemes representing SNCB, DB and SNCF house colours respectively, apart from the yellow end panels on the DB locomotive.

STAGE 3.
Trainload Freight: The three schemes for this sector were as follows:

Mainline: A medium-blue body with white strip along the centre, the word 'Mainline' below this halfway along the body, with a white circle with double white-striped circles emanating from the central circle. Cab surrounds, doors, roofs, chassis and other equipment all in black. White numbers under the nearside cab windows and repeated in blue off-centre on the yellow front end. A number of locomotives retained two-tone grey. These were embellished with the circular Mainline circles in blue and yellow surrounds, with the word 'Mainline' in black.

Loadhaul: Black bodysides, cab surrounds, roofs and other equipment were enhanced by orange areas below the cab sides extending around the front just into the yellow front end. Black numbers (omitting the class) applied to the yellow ends, and the full number in black under the nearside cab. A plaque comprising a top half in white, with the word 'Load' in black, and a bottom half in grey with the word 'Haul' in white, with a thin orange letter 'L' at the bottom left-hand corner, was applied below cantrail height, two-thirds along the length of the engine. Three Class 60s remained in two-tone grey, having the Loadhaul plaque applied in line with other sector members.

Transrail: Locomotives remained in two-tone grey, but without sector decals. A white capital 'T' on a blue background, surrounded by red and white bands, underlined by two red stripes, was applied to the bodyside off-centre according to the class, with the word 'Transrail' in white capital letters alongside. A red repeater strip was applied to the opposite end cab door.

Private Companies: Yeoman, ARC, National Power, Hunslet Barclay and DRS all had their own company schemes.
At privatisation in 1996, European Passenger Services continued in their two-tone grey scheme with roundels, as did Yeoman, ARC (which became Hanson) and DRS in their own schemes. All other schemes are gradually repainted into EWS 'Wisconsin Central' red and cream, or, in the case of Freightliner, into their own corporate green colours are used apart from a few Class 90s, which still retain the original grey with red triangles.

Examples of all these liveries and many of the variations are illustrated in this volume.

LOCOMOTIVE NAMES

A large number of locomotives in the freight and departmental sectors carried a far-reaching selection of names during

Above:
An example of a plate with supplementary plates giving further information. No 31107 has two extra plates, with the name of *John H. Carless* set on a dark blue background.

this period of review. Many names were applied, some transferred between engines, and some dispensed with altogether.

The names were carried on cast steel or aluminium plates, using both block capital or lower case letters in line with BR standard practice, although there were inevitable variations. For example, No 20173 *Wensleydale* had its name painted on the frame, whilst No 47079 *G. J. Churchward*, one of the GW150 engines, had a nameplate cast in brass in the style of the old Great Western Railway, with letters to suit. The four Freight connection Class 90s had a different script from the BR standard lettering.

Many of the names relating to industry were embellished with logos appertaining to the industrial group, such as coal mining, or to a particular company such as No 56124 *Blue Circle Cement* and No 56132 *Fina Energy*.

The size of the nameplates obviously varied from small to very large, in the latter case an example being *County of West Glamorgan/Sir Gorliewin Morgannwg* which needed two lines on a full-length plate.

Certain engines carried nameplates relating to a particular event or person, and these often carried ancillary plates giving additional information. The photo of the nameplate of *John H. Carless* illustrates this well.

An exception to the cast nameplates was the Class 92, on which, with the exception of two (post-privatisation four) engines which carried normal plates, the names were stencilled. The two exceptions are No 92022 *Charles Dickens* and No 92023 *Ravel*.

In the majority of cases, the backgrounds of the plates were either red or black, but there were a few in blue, and the background for No 50149 was a unique yellow.

Examples of the range of subjects covered within the different locomotive classes include:

Class 20 – Associations with North East England, girls' names (Hunslet Barclay).

Class 31 – Preserved railways, associations with Bescot TMD and the Black Country.

Class 33 – Aircraft associated with the Eastleigh/Southampton area, Earl Mountbatten, Channel Tunnel activity locations.

Class 37 – British Steel plants, motive power depots, industrial associations, Welsh counties, school trophy winners, famous people, etc.

Class 47 – Industrial organisations, famous people, transport organisations, military groups, etc.

Class 50 – Warship (*Defiance*).

Class 56 – Welsh counties, power stations, industrial organisations, people, institutions, Crewe Locomotive works, etc.

Class 58 – Collieries, power stations, TMDs.

Class 59 – Yeoman 'Aspirations', North Somerset villages, English and Welsh vales.

Class 60 – Mountains, famous people.

Class 73 – Preserved railways, places or other aspects associated with the Southern Region.

Class 86 – Institutions, famous people, etc.

Class 87 – Stephenson.

Class 90 – Freight connections with European Railways.

Class 92 – European authors and musicians.

Freightliner Class 47 and 90 – Intermodal centres.

Web site www.therailwaycentre.com shows full coverage of all nameplates with engine numbers, dates of application and other details.

DEPOT MASCOT PLATES

Under the second phase of Railfreight sectorisation, distinctive emblems were introduced to give a sense of pride for employees in regard to the locomotives allocated to particular engine sheds, and for their care and identification.

This feature followed what had been unofficial identification marks adopted by certain sheds during the first phase. In the first instance, St Blazey shed had marked two Class 37 engines with Cornish Rail markings, but this approach was carried much further, using white or coloured stickers, by the following:

> Stratford – *Cockney Sparrow*
> Thornaby – *Kingfisher*
> Eastfield – *Scottish Terrier*
> Shields Road – *Salmon (for Class 81)*
> Inverness – *Highland Stag*

The second phase was far expanded from this initial concept, virtually all locations having their own unique identification in the form of cast aluminium plates. Locomotive depots as well as wagon repair shops were covered, and are outlined below.

LOCOMOTIVE DEPOTS:

Bescot – *Saddle*
Buxton – *Millstone*
Cardiff – *Goat*
Crewe Diesel – *Cheshire Cat*
Crewe Electric – *Eagle*

Right:
The Stratford Cockney Sparrow logo is decked out in a footplateman's cab and waistcoat.

Eastfield – *Scottish Terrier*
Eastleigh – *Spitfire*
Hither Green – *Oasthouses*
Immingham – *Star of the East*
Laira – *Mayflower Ship*
Leicester – *Panther*
Motherwell – *Hammer and Anvil*
Ripple Lane – *Flaming Torch*
Saltley – *Seagull*
St Blazey – *Lizard*
Stewarts Lane – *Battersea Power Station*
Stratford – *Cockney Sparrow*
Thornaby – *Kingfisher*
Toton – *Power Station Cooling Towers*
Westbury – *White Horse*
Willesden – *Greyhound*

WAGON REPAIR SHOPS:

Barry – *Galleon*
Carlisle Currock – *Fox*
Grangemouth – *Galleon*
Ipswich – *Suffolk Punch Horse*
Knottingley – *Pit Winding Gear*
Margam – *Kite (bird of prey)*
Southampton – *Ocean Liner*

The mascot plates for the Wagon Repair depots were used on a few wagons in some cases, but were primarily used to identify the depot.

The choice of emblem was in most cases submitted by the depot staff, and had a relationship with either the type of traffic or an area association. For example, Motherwell's Hammer and Anvil related to traffic to and from the nearby Ravenscraig steelworks for which the depot provided traction. Eastleigh's Spitfire recalled the Supermarine aircraft works in nearby Southampton.

Comprehensive details of these and a few other miscellaneous emblems can be seen on the railway centre website.

RAILFREIGHT AND DEPARTMENTAL ROLLING STOCK

Apart from the locomotives themselves, a very wide range of standard and specialist freight wagons were in use during the period from sectorisation to privatisation.

At the beginning of the period, a few vacuum-braked wagons were still operating, but by the end of it, all vehicles were air-braked. Particular vacuum-braked favourites were the China Clay Hoods and the bogie hoppers used by ICI for services from Tunstead Quarry. Brake vans were used at the start with nuclear flask traffic, but this was no longer necessary with time. Brake vans are still used in departmental work on occasions, especially when propelling moves take place, and some are adapted with ploughs for spreading ballast.

To survey the freight wagons requires a book on its own, and the reader is recommended to visit the web site 'Wagons on the Web', which gives comprehensive information and illustrations of almost every type of vehicle.

For the purposes of this publication, a list of the TOPS category and some well-known examples of wagons are shown.

B	*Bogie Steel Carriers*
BAA	*Steel Bar Carriers*
C	*Cov Hops & Brake Vans*
CDA	*2 Axle China Clay Hopper*
F	*2 Axle & Bogie Flat Wagons*
FCA	*Freightliner Bogie Flat*
H	*2 Axle & Bogie Hoppers*
HAA	*2 Axle Coal Hopper*
J	*Bogie Private Owners Wagons*
JHA	*Bogie Aggregate Wagon*
K	*Private Owner Special Wagons*
KWA	*MOD 'Warwell' Well Wagon*

Above:
Mainline Grey No 60083 *Shining Tor* leaves Twerton Tunnel near Bath with the Furzebrook to Hallen Marsh LPG tanks. August 1996.

M	*2 Axle & Bogie Mineral Wagons*
MEA	*2 Axle Box Open Wagon*
O	*2 Axle Open Wagons*
OTA	*2 Axle Timber Wagon*
P	*2 Axle Private Owners Wagons*
PCA	*2 Axle Presflo Wagons*
S	*2 Axle Steel Carriers*
SPA	*2 Axle Low Sided Steel Carrier*
T	*2 Axle & Bogie Tank Wagons*
TTA	*2 Axle Tank Wagon*
W	*Special Wagons*
WIA	*Double Deck Car Carrier*
Y	*Bogie Departmental Stock*
YBA	*'Sturgeon' Rail/Sleeper Carrier*
Z	*2 Axle Departmental Stock*
ZBO	*'Grampus' 2 Axle Spoil/General Materials Wagon*

Examples of many types of freight and departmental wagons are shown in the illustrations herein.

SUMMARY

This book has outlined what has happened during the 13 years from Railfreight becoming a separately identified organisation within British Rail up to the privatisation of the railways.

Throughout this period, the freight businesses have continued to develop more cost- effective, customer-related operations, without having the perceived glamour of the passenger sector. At the outset, freight services were operated using a varied selection of early diesel and electric locomotive classes, hauling relatively short trains primarily geared to the manufacturing sector. But over the period under review, the decline of British manufacturing operations, the effects of the coal miners' strike in the 1980s, and the increase in imported goods have changed the freight scene substantially. In addition, since privatisation, the influx of illegal immigrants from France using Channel Tunnel freight services and the charges for using the Tunnel have all but eliminated this source of traffic. Thus, at the time of writing this book, the regular services are less frequent than before, are generally longer and, with the exception of nuclear services, are in the hands of only three major locomotive classes – Nos 60, 66 and 90 — with limited support from Classes Nos 56, 86 and 92.

For the historian and model maker, there will be a great interest in how and why things have changed, and undoubtedly how developments will continue to take place over the forthcoming years. Privatisation has provided opportunities that have been seized by the different freight companies, and they have, in the main, succeeded in attracting and developing new business upon the foundation of what still remains of the traditional rail freight. In terms of business levels, the road-to-rail ratio for ton-miles of freight handled of over 11:1 previously, has reduced to a little over 7:1. Let us hope that this progress continues to germinate and develop.

I think it is appropriate, therefore, to conclude by saluting the various employees at all levels, with their traditions of loyal service, who have achieved all this without any widespread recognition, and more often than not in unsocial conditions.

Below:
One of the two locomotives used on the Isle of Wight in January1990, No 03079 stands waiting for business with its departmental train at Sandown. The other locomotive was No 03179 painted in NSE colours.

Bottom:
Class 08 No 08620 shunts the Blue Circle depot at Grangemouth in March 1987. The train comprises standard PCA cement wagons. This depot is alongside Grangemouth shed, very convenient for my visits to the depot!

Left:
A pair of Class 20s, with No 20204 leading, head a train of gypsum wagons from the British Plasterboard plant at Kirby Thore, and cement empties from the BCC Uddingston (View Park) depot to the works at Oxwellmains. The train is nearing Dunbar in May 1986.

Below:
One of the chemical sub-sector '25/9s', No 25901 pulls empties out of BCCs Carlisle depot at Upperby in March 1987. This depot was built within the remains of the old LNWR/LMS shed.

Above:
An unidentified Class 27 brings a variety of freight wagons past the old Freightliner depot and carriage sidings at Portobello on its way to Millerhill in April 1986. Note the Scottish Terrier decal on the locomotive, signifying that it is shedded at Eastfield.

Right:
A pair of Class 31s, the lead locomotive in BR blue, the trailing one in Railfreight livery, head a train of eastbound oil tanks near Mirfield in March 1987.

Right:
No 33012 and No 33008 *Eastleigh*, restored to its original green livery, but with the addition of yellow warning panels, bring a ballast train into Chichester yard in April 1989. Rationalisation of the track now means that trains have to reverse into the yard from this direction; such is progress.

Above:
Not a shot available to the public. No 33202 waits at Blue Circle's Northfleet works whilst its train of gypsum from Mountfield is unloaded. The front number shows signs of being painted somewhat unprofessionally. March 1986.

Left:
One of those services that came and went, and one was glad to get shot of it at the time. The load will hardly tax No 37320, with its Didcot to Totton SCN coal service passing Silchester in June 1988.

Right:
A pair of Class 37s, both with split headcodes, approach West Thurrock Junction with a Freightliner from Ripple Lane to Tilbury in September 1987. Access to this site was from a footpath at the BCC Wouldham depot which is now closed.

Right:
An unidentified Class 45 heads north near Claydon with coal empties from Blue Circle's Masons works to Thoresby colliery. OHE installed as far as Stowmarket at this stage. May 1986.

Below:
A blue Class 47 speeds an up freight train through East Linton in May 1986. The train has a mix of a one grain wagon, several vans and auto carriers.

Left:

No 47225 starts to accelerate away from passing under the LSW mainline at Culvert Road junction, with a Willesden to Dover Speedlink service in April 1989. Another location where the track layout has since been modified.

Left:

In July 1984, driver training for air-braked locomotive haulage took place at Eastleigh depot. Class 405 4SUBs were used as the load, and in this view, a set of three, the rear one of which was unit No 4742, were hauled on an Eastleigh, Southampton, Laverstock, Basingstoke, Eastleigh circuit. Blue No 56047 is photographed at Whitchurch, making a unique picture.

Below:

Class 56 No 56004 was repainted in BR blue and retained as one of the heritage fleet. It is seen here in May 1996 at Worting Junction, with the Quidhampton to Willesden Calcium Carbonate working, coming off the Salisbury line.

Right:
A long since gone working seen here approaching Woking by St John's Golf Club. The train, headed by a Class 73, is an MOD service from Aldershot Military Sidings travelling, I think, to Willesden. April 1985.

Above:
With diesel engines working hard, a pair of Class 73s struggle to get moving from Hoo Junction up yard with a train of Auto racks. It is April 1986, and the locomotives are No 73133 in BR large logo colours, and No 73122 *County of East Sussex* in original Mainline livery.

Right:
Class 81 No 81012 brings a train of UKF fertilizer wagons from Ince past the overbridge near Winwick Junction in March 1987. These locomotives were used for mixed traffic duties. Note the leaping salmon logo, indicating that it was a Shields Road locomotive at that time.

Right:
Not many shunting locomotives were painted in sector colours. This example, Class 08, No 08805, looked very smart whilst acting as station pilot at Birmingham New Street in April 1986. Note the number painted on the front buffer beam, and the outsize Railfreight name.

Above:
Bescot shed was one which liked to do a non-standard paint job on some of its allocation. This example, No 08832, is seen with double white lines and an oversize number. Railfreight label in available space on the cab side, and a small blue BS shed label underneath. It was shunting outside Bescot shed in July 1987. Note the lamp carried on the front steps — something seen quite often on shunting locomotives.

Left:
An unidentified Railfreight '31' brings a short freight across the points at the north end of York station in March 1987.

Right:
A pair of 31s wait between duties in Buxton station in February 1986. Large snowplough at each end with No 31210 nearest the camera.

Below:
A pair of 31s, No 31199 in original Railfreight and No 31188 in Railfreight Red Stripe, pass the remains of the old Midland Railway shed at Stourton in March 1989. The train is comprised of Tilcon stone wagons.

Bottom:
A bird's-eye view of Lostwithiel station in the pouring rain. Typical June weather in 1987! No 37674 starts its run down to Carne Point with a load of China Clay hoods, with more loads waiting in the sidings. This view remains virtually unchanged apart from the trains, with signalbox and semaphore signals still in situ.

Above:
No 37512 *Thornaby Demon* in standard Railfreight, and No 37506 *British Steel Skinningrove* in Red Stripe livery bring the Lackenby to Corby steel coils past Grangetown in February 1988. A typical heavy industrial scene in the North East illustrating the rationale for which the railways were originally developed in the 19th Century.

Left:
Not a very bright day, but worth recording this train at Wisbech in March 1986.
No 47379 has been tarted up with full red buffer beams and buffers, and is about to leave for March after servicing the Metal Box Company's operations in this town.

Left:
A view at Greave's Sidings with No 47237 in standard Railfreight livery waiting with a rake of MOD vans from Fenny Compton, whilst in the distance the Blue Circle Sentinel locomotive shunts cement wagons to be attached to the rear of the train. May 1988.

Right:
A rather dirty No 47095 brings the St Blazey to Cliffe Vale China Clay working past the LNWR signalbox at Wednesbury in June 1989. The crossover provides access to the link line up to the old GWR line to Wolverhampton on which Wednesbury steel terminal remains.

Below:
No 56057 smokes the night away on Canton shed in January 1987. Note the remains of a Class 47 body propped up on sleepers, the sort of thing a modeller might incorporate into a layout.

Left:
Completely standard Railfreight Class 56 No 56066 brings a fully loaded MGR train of coal from the West Midlands collieries over Foxhall Junction on its way to serve Didcot Power Station in May 1986.

Below left:
A pair of '56s' with the biggest nameplates on BR at that time haul another load of iron ore from Port Talbot to Llanwern steelworks past Cardiff Canton in June 1987.
The locomotives are No 56053 *County of Mid Glamorgan* and No 56032 *County of South Glamorgan*, plus the Welsh versions of these names.

Below:
Another pair of '56s', this time on the loop line at Theale with stone empties. No 56034 *Ogmore Castle* is in Railfreight, whilst No 56042 is in BR blue. The latter locomotive is of particular interest, being fitted with prototype bogies which were to be used on the Class 58s. The date is September 1985.

RAILFREIGHT
RED STRIPE

Left:
A dull day at Thornaby, with No 20165 *Henry Pease* standing in the shed yard in February 1988. Nameplates attached at front end of frame as on other Class 20s with cast names. Thornaby Kingfisher shed logo on hood. For the modeller, note the yellow axle box covers and white coil springs. The railfreight plate is cast and not a decal.

Above:
The classic East Midlands coal working, as a pair of Class 20s, nose to nose, bring an MGR past the signalbox at Welbeck Colliery Junction. The lead locomotive in Red Stripe colours is No 20165, and the date is May 1986.

Right:
The view from the A52 at Toton in July 1988, when the yards were still reasonably busy. No 20108 and No 20215, both in Red Stripe livery, head north with a trainload of ballast, past the points giving access to the locomotive shed. The headcode discs show up nicely on a pair of clean engines.

Above:
No 26035 shunts Blue Circle's Aberdeen depot at Craiginches in July 1988. The red stripe is covered in dirt! Full size Eastfield Scottish Terrier logo on the body side.

Left:
No 26040 stands in Irvine station on a wet day in March 1987, with an overhead electrification train. Note the snowploughs fitted to the locomotive.

Left:
A signal gantry at the platform ends of Norwich station frames the arrival of a Whitemoor to Norwich Speedlink service in June 1987. The train is headed by a nice clear Red Stripe No 31268.

Right:
A Thornaby depot special. No 31327 *Phillips-Imperial* is seen on Ripple Lane shed in October 1987. Non-standard white large logo number on body side, repeated above buffer beam, Thornaby Kingfisher shed logo, and company crests underneath nameplate.

Above:
A sparkling clean No 31276 shows off the Red Stripe colours as it enters the yards at Thornaby with a train of VTG cargo vans. Chemical industry dominates the background in March 1987.

Right:
Split headcode No 37353 and BR blue No 37038 speed through the yards at Ely with a Parkeston to Doncaster Speedlink service in May 1989. Note the decimated semaphore posts, the South signalbox roof, and the Class 47 waiting in the sidings to follow this train.

Above:
The tide is out at Golant as No 37672
Freight Transport Association heads along the
causeway with a load of China Clay to be
unloaded at Carne Point. April 1988.

Left:
No 37502 *British Steel Teesside* in Railfreight
Red Stripe leads No 37501*Teesside
Steelmaster* in its unique light blue British
Steel large logo colour scheme with dark blue
backed nameplate. The down train of steel
sections is just entering the four-track section
of the ECML at Ouston Junction in June
1988. Electrification masts have yet to be
erected.

Left:
The St Blazey to Gloucester Speedlink
service comprising a mixture of wagons
handling China Clay products is on the
approach to Moorswater viaduct in April
1988. Two of the St Blazey '37' fleet are in
charge — No 37672 *Freight Transport
Association* and unnamed No 37674, both in
clean Railfreight Red Stripe colours.

Right:
Non-freight duty for No 47249 as it stops in Reading platform 5 with an unidentified express in August 1987. The Railfreight Red Stripe contrasts unhappily with the blue and grey mark 1 coaching stock. The scaffolding indicates that the overbridge was starting to be erected at this date.

Above:
No 47227 has lost its Railfreight label from the cabside, as it heads south at Aynho Junction with a Crewe to Southampton Maritime Freightliner in July 1991.

Right:
Another non-standard locomotive, this time No 47363 *Billingham Enterprise*, which sits out the day on Saltley shed in March 1989. The red stripe does not extend around the cabs and front end, and the white number is large logo size under the nameplate instead of being standard black on the cab side. The crest above the nameplate and Thornaby's Kingfisher add to the details.

Left:
Plastered in red all around the front end, No 56019 brings a trainload of coal from the West Midlands bound for Didcot Power Station. Otherwise the locomotive is in standard Red Stripe livery. Greave's Sidings in May 1988.

Above:
Standard Red Stripe liveried No 56100 hauls a fully loaded MGR from the Selby coalfield to one of the Aire Valley power stations. The location is Burton Salmon, and the date is July 1991.

Left:
Pretty much straight out of Doncaster works, No 58002 displays the full effect of the Red Stripe scheme at the open day held at Stratford in July 1983. Patience needed to avoid too many spotters in the picture!

Above:
No 58042 is seen here at Codnor Park in July 1987, with an MGR service heading for Toton. The nameplate *Ironbridge Power Station* with British Coal logo in the top left hand corner (see miscellaneous photo section) replaces the Railfreight adhesive label, which in turn has been replaced by a cast Railfreight plate on the front end.

Below:
A less common duty for a Class 58. No 58007 and blue No 47330 are taking a Lawley Street to Holyhead Freightliner along the roundabout route through Sutton Park, as it approaches Ryecroft Junction in August 1989.

COAL SECTOR

Right:
A pair of Class 26s run light engine through the yards at Mossend on their way to Ravenscraig steel works. It is February 1989 and the locomotives are No 26007 and No 26008. Note the absence of Depot Mascot plates and BR double arrows.

Left:
Class 31 No 31324 is banking a southbound train of LPG tanks past Landor Street Junction up the gradient towards St Andrews Junction and Camp Hill. BR double arrow on left hand cab side, abbreviated number on front end, Depot Mascot plate for Crewe Diesel depot on right hand cab side. March 1989.

Below:
Rather grubby, Crewe Diesel depot allocated No 31199 in full Coal sector colours leaves the Salt Union works with a Weston Point to Runcorn trip working in January 1994.

Above:
No 37799 *County of Dyfed* has the right sector scheme for handling Cawoods coal containers as it comes off the line from the Welsh Marches at Maindee West Junction in February 1991. Standard coal colours, but no Depot Mascot plate.

Right:
No 37274 has charge of the coal service from Didcot which serves yards at Neasden, Purley and Hove. With autumn tints brightening a cloudy day, the train is approaching Tilehurst in November 1989. An oversize number is placed on the RHS on the nose, but a Depot Mascot plate is missing.

Right:
Quite what a coal sector '56' and a train of MGR empties was doing on the line at Park Royal in October 1989, I don't know. The locomotive was No 56015. Central line tracks on the right, and out of sight on the left was the siding into the Guiness Park Royal brewery, which at that time was still in use.

Above:
MGR empties head back north behind Coal sector No 56094, which lacks a Depot Mascot plate and BR double arrow emblem. This view is at Chaloners Whin, where the old ECML came in on the left — note the wooden fence on the left showing the old alignment. Also note that somebody doesn't know how to spell Toilet (sic)!

Left:
A nice pairing of two coal sector classes with MGR empties from Didcot Power Station heading back to the Midlands at the classic viewpoint near King's Sutton. It is July 1991, and the engines are No 56018 and No 58030, both clean and in full dress.

Left:
A February day dawns bright at Oxford in 1991 as Class 58 No 58043 drags its load of coal through the station on its way to Didcot Power Station. The locomotive is in full coal sector colours, with a Toton Depot Mascot plate.

Right:
A '58' line-up on Saltley shed in March 1989. Sparkling No 58015 heads Red Stripe No 58007, and in the rear is coal sector No 58014 *Didcot Power Station* being attended by the shed fitters. No 58015 lacks a Depot mascot plate, but note the two red diamond coupling codes.

Right:
Didcot Power Station, No 58014, is seen again, this time framed by the up signal gantry at Aynho Junction, as it takes another load of coal to Didcot in July 1991. Trains due in both directions to keep me occupied!

Below:
Clean No 60069 *Humphrey Davy* takes the down fast at Sharnbrook with Bardon coloured empties from Hayes to Mountsorrel on a Saturday in October 1991. No Depot Mascot plate.

Above:
The August 1991 open day at Old Oak Common shed provided for a special working throughout the day to and from Paddington via the Greenford loop. Here we see No 60047 *Robert Owen*, topped-and-tailed with Yeoman No 59005 *Kenneth J. Painter*, passing the Central Line flying junctions at North Acton. The headboard says *Greenford Grinder*. No Depot Mascot.

Below:
The days when the Channel Tunnel was being constructed (May 1991), with much traffic being provided by BR. No 60046 *William Wilberforce* clatters over the points serving the Hastings line at Tonbridge with empties from Sevington to Cliffe. 2EPB and 4CAP units parked in the sidings.

CONSTRUCTION SECTOR

Left:
Two of the relatively rare Construction sector Class 31s bring the Stewartby to Stonebridge Park empties past Hunton Bridge as they approach the north end of Watford Tunnel in March 1990. The wagons have been used to take contaminated soil from Chatham Dockyard to the worked out clay pits of the London Brick Company. The locomotives are No 31271 and No 31294, both with Bescot depot Mascot plates.

Above:
Towards the closure of the Dunkirk–Dover train ferry service, No 33207 *Earl Mountbatten of Burma* is taking VTG Cargo vans off the ship to be stabled in Dover yard for a while. The locomotive has a Hither Green Depot Mascot plate. Note the red and white headcode blinds, which saves having to change them every time there is a shunting move. The location is at Dover Western Docks.

Right:
The Sevington–Cliffe empties in this example are hauled by a pair of Class 33s, No 33050 *Isle of Grain* and unnamed No 33021. The train is at Hoo Junction in August 1989. Neither engine carries a Depot Mascot plate, and the #5 headcode is suspect. Scenery by courtesy of South Thamesside!

Left:
No 33064 rounds the bend into Shalford station with a Woking to Tonbridge departmental working. The date is July 1993, the sun is shining and all is well. No headcode is carried and at which shed the locomotive is based in unknown.

Below:
With signals off for the loop down to Acton yard, No 37178 and No 37354 bring the Harlow to Acton empties past Acton Wells signalbox on a dull lunchtime in January 1989.

Above:
Another classic location at Arpley, with Warrington Bank Quay Station and the chemical works dominating the background. No 37681 in Construction sector colours and No 37679 in Railfreight Red Stripe livery are hauling a train of stone empties in February 1990.

Right:
A shot for the modellers of No 47901, the re-engined one, stabled at Westbury in April 1988. Standard Construction livery colours, but non-standard front number. Cardiff depot plate shows up clearly. Note how the blue area at the top left of the construction blue and yellow squares forms a letter 'F' shape for Freight. This can also be seen with Metals and Petroleum sector decals, but less clearly with Coal and Railfreight Distribution schemes.

Right:
The empties from Forders Sidings at Stewartby have been diverted on their way back to Chatham Dockyard, due to the line closure at Kensington Olympia. They are seen here at Barnes, in charge of No 56103 in November 1992. Note the sheeting over the wagons, which had carried the contaminated soil.

Above:
A shot that is now impossible, taken from the old signalbox at North Pole Junction. No 56032 *County of South Glamorgan* is climbing the bank from the GW main line with a Whatley to Chiselhurst stone train in May 1989. This line had, until recently, given access to the Eurostar depot. The wagons are ARC owned, which was correct for a train from Whatley, before the days of merged stone traffic from the Mendips.

Left:
On display at the Bescot open day in May 1990, No 56062 *Mountsorrel* stands proudly in the sun with a rake of Redland self-discharge train wagons. Taken early in the day, so no spotters in the way!

Left:
Sometimes it helps when the sun is not out, which enables a picture to be taken from the wrong side. In this case, un-mascotted No 60041 *High Willhays* is in charge of the diverted Calvert to Westerleigh Bin Liner on the down main at Lower Basildon. The date is July 1993.

Above:

Another location to which public access is now precluded, unless special permission is obtained. No 60099 *Ben More Assynt* is at Helpston in June 1993, with a Redland self-discharge train, presumably returning to Mountsorrel for another load. A perfect June day with lots of trains, and no Class 66s!

Below:

At a location where I have spent many hundreds of hours, Potbridge, the autumn sun nicely lights the pioneer Class 60, No 60001 *Steadfast* as it trundles along the up relief line with its train of stone from Whatley to Woking. Hither Green Depot Mascot plate, and blinds down against the low sun. November 1992.

METALS SECTOR

Right:
Standard haulage in July 1990 for the Port Talbot to Llanwern iron ore trains. Seen at Pencoed are No 37905 *Vulcan Enterprise* and No 37884. Although without Mascot plates, they must be Cardiff engines.

Above:
No 37710 is missing a front number as it leads No 37884 back to Port Talbot after taking its load of iron ore to Llanwern. It is about to go under the branch from Tondu at Margam in July 1990. Again, they are probably Cardiff locomotives, but Canton shed seems to enjoy anonymity!

Left:
No 37671 *Tre Pol and Pen* is seen here in its short-lived Metals sector colours, before it was re-decalled to join its St Blazey friends Nos 37670 and 37672-5 in Railfreight Distribution livery. The train is a Tavistock Junction to St Blazey Speedlink service, the location is Wearde and the date April 1989. The rain has cleared, but has it washed off the front number?

Right:
No 37507 *Hartlepool Pipe Mill* displays the full range of Metals Sector colours, including the sector strip by the cab door, but with a non-standard front number. The nameplate and Thornaby's Kingfisher motif can be seen in detail in the miscellaneous section. Parked with a Trans-Pennine coach at Thornaby shed in February 1988.

Above:
Not normal work for a Metals 47, but a summer Saturday Manchester to Poole train needed something. No 47594 makes for the coast through the New Forest near Lyndhurst Road in August 1990. Happy holidays!

Right:
More for the model makers, as ultra clean No 47347 ambles through Doncaster station. An absolutely standard colour scheme, and a whiff of black exhaust to add to the pollution in August 1988.

Top:
Well it ought to be a Coal sector locomotive, but Metals sector No 56043 does a stirling job taking an MGR train to either Eggborough or Drax Power Stations. Taken at Whitley Bridge in August 1994. Is the driver's tea getting cold in the teapot?

Above:
A broadside view of No 56061 as it heads towards West Drayton with its trainload of coal from Coedbach in February 1998. Depot Mascot Plate missing. The scene is near Ruscombe.

Left:
Standard Metals sector No 60038 *Bidean Nam Bian* brings the Corby to Lackenby steel empties under the road bridge at Burton Salmon in April 1991. Clean locomotive, dull day.

Above:
Unnamed No 60031 brings the Cliffe Vale to St Blazey China Clay empties past the holiday camp at Dawlish Warren in July 1990, in the days when there was still quite a lot of locomotive hauled traffic on this line. Depot Mascot Plate washed out and therefore unintelligible.

Below:
It ought to be a Petroleum sector locomotive, but Metals No 60049 *Scafell* is doing a good job as it passes through Nottingham station with empty Total tanks returning to Lindsey refinery. The clean locomotive has no Depot Mascot plate. Seen in July 1991.

PETROLEUM SECTOR

Right:
As this and the next photo show, Immingham depot was not noted for keeping its Class 31s clean. The modelmaker can see how to weather his locomotive, in this case No 31319 taking empty tanks back from Gainsborough to Lindsey, as it passes through Lincoln in April 1992.

Left:
No 31319 is seen again, this time with No 31302, and still dirty, as it passes Barnetby station with empties for Lindsey refinery. March 1992. Both locomotives display Immingham's Star of the East Mascot plates.

Below:
A foggy day in London town, where No 37705 lives up to its name as it shunts a few tanks at Ripple Lane. The flaming torch Depot Mascot plate shows up, as does the full number on the nose of the locomotive. October 1989.

Above:
The evening sun lights up Blackford's semaphores and the Inverness to Millerhill Speedlink, which is headed by No 37708. This service almost always contained oil tanks from Inverness shed and cement wagons from BCC Inverness depot for returning to Oxwellmains works. April 1991.

Right:
It is an evening in April 1991, and Dundee basks in the evening sun as a Metals sector Class 47 (take my word for it) takes the Oxwellmains to Dundee/Aberdeen BCC depots train over the Tay Bridge.

Right:
One of the batch of 47s allocated specially for petroleum duties, black headcoded No 47054 *Xenodiae*, takes a load of tanks through the crossovers at Colton Junction in July 1991. The front number has just enough space to be squeezed in under the headcode panel.

Above:
Only one Class 56 received Petroleum sector decals — by mistake? Unique No 56036 is seen at Kensal Green Junction in January 1989 returning its empty stone wagons to Whatley. Front number is rather oversize.

Left:
The Kensington Olympia blockade in November 1992 forced the diversion of the Llandarcy–Grain tanks, which are seen here behind No 60024 *Elizabeth Fry* at Ascot, shortly before the autumn leaves fall.

Below:
Before all the pipelines were built to serve Heathrow, No 60064 *Back Tor* passes the Plasser and Thauer works at West Ealing with empty tanks returning to Lindsey from Langley. The date is May 1992, and the footbridge has not yet been netted in.

Left:
The unique RFD Class 31 No 31160 stands outside Bescot shed at the open day in May 1990. The locomotive has been named *Phoenix* using a Tinsley label, and displays the Tinsley Depot Mascot plate. Very low front number due to the position of the front light and lamp brackets.

Right:
Two of the only five Class 33s with RFD decals, No 33205 and No 33203, wait outside the Blue Circle depot at Theale, ready to return the empties to Northfleet works. Note the very small cabside numbers and no Depot Mascot plates. At least one of these five was numbered temporarily in '33/3' series, eg No 33302 which was on display at the Winchfield open day.

Below:
The sun is shining, the daffodils are out, and St Blazey allocated No 37673 climbs past Treesmill with its Goonbarrow to Carne Point China Clay train. St Blazey Lizard Mascot plate on the side of the cab. March 1990

Above:
The light is starting to fade as No 37673 and No 37670 take their St Blazey to Gloucester Speedlink service past Starcross in June 1990. No front number on the lead locomotive. Brunel's atmospheric pumping station in the distance. All in all a super time at a classic location.

Left:
I make no excuses for showing another RFD '37' in the West Country. In this case No 37412 is taking a Moorswater to Carne Point train round a curve near Liskeard in November 1990. The low sun lights up the dirt on the bodyside, so modellers please note how to do it.

Left:
March 1990 at Exminster, where No 47144 is seen with the oil tank service to Heathfield. The crew of two enjoy the morning sun, Exeter Cathedral is seen on the skyline. Note the white diamond between the marker lights.

Right:
A summer Saturday in June 1989, and No 47588 *Carlisle Currock* is bringing a train from Wolverhampton under the M27 near Paulsgrove on its way to Portsmouth Harbour. Large front number, but otherwise standard colours.

Right:
The usual pairing of Class 86s with a Freightliner train, shows No 86609 and No 86613 *County of Lancashire* passing South Kenton with a service from Felixstowe in August 1993. An express approaches in the distance, and a Watford–Euston train disappears into North Wembley station.

Right:
No 86609 and No 86631 haul an unidentified Freightliner through Wolverton Station in May 1995. Crewe Electric Depot Mascot plate on both locomotives.

Left:
Another unique RFD engine, this time fairly short-lived in this scheme. A rather grubby No 87101 *Stephenson* shows itself at the open day at Worksop in September 1993. Crewe Electric mascot plate, no front number, stainless steel nameplate and OHL warning labels behind cab doors.

Left:
The prototype locomotive used for the Railfreight Distribution colour scheme was a Class 90. No 90136 is seen running light engine at Headstone Lane in March 1993. Of particular interest is the full orange end, the words 'Railfreight Distribution' in red in the light grey bodyside band, and the half-height RFD repeater strip by the cab door.

Below:
In contrast to the previous picture, a well worn '90', No 90139, is seen at Hatch End with a Dover to Crewe Basford Hall freight, containing a good mix of wagons. The old main line island platform remains are still in situ, and access to the down main platform is still available in June 1993, but the old crossovers, semaphores and signalbox which used to be here have long gone.

RAILFREIGHT DISTRIBUTION

Right:

The European version of RFD is displayed in its full glory on No 47033 *Royal Logistics Corps*. The words 'Railfreight Distribution' are placed in the light grey bodyside band. The White Rose of Tinsley depot gleams and the depot has done a magnificent job preparing it for display at the May 1995 open day at Rickmansworth.

Right:

Very much more work-stained than that above is No 47053 *Dollands Moor International*, which is taking its Ford 'Blue Train' from Dagenham to Dollands Moor, then to Spain, past Otford Junction. February 1998.

Below:

RFDE No 86622 and No 86615 *Rotary International*, devoid of decals, take a northbound Freightliner past Slindon in May 1995. Not much revenue on this service. Cow in unusual pose, looking right — they normally look over their left shoulders!

Left:
No 90133 and RES liveried No 86424 are stabled at Crewe in March 1994. The '90' is missing the words 'Railfreight Distribution' from the bodyside, but the contrast between the dark grey and light grey body colours shows up well.

Left:
No 90134 takes the down main at Headstone Lane with a trainload of Dagenham to Halewood car carriers in May 1995. Nice clean locomotive in full RFDE colours with white fittings around the bogies.

Below:
Before the Class 92s were commissioned for service, and trains bound for the Channel Tunnel were hauled by pairs of RFDE Class 47s, which were prohibited from transit through the Tunnel, a small batch of French locomotives were used to take trains from Dollands Moor through to Calais etc. SNCF Class BB22200 No 22379 is seen stabled at Dollands Moor in July 1994. The standard French grey and orange paint scheme has been embellished with a yellow nose (BR safety requirement), an orange strip on the buffer beam, a mini RFD decal and words 'Railfreight Distribution', and the letters TTU by the number.

Below:
Another unique locomotive, the Class 50 fitted with freight bogies, is seen here at Westbury in October 1987. No 50149

Defiance is taking No 56048 in large logo livery to Cardiff Canton shed. Details of the cab end of this engine can be seen in the miscellaneous section

Below:
No 50149 *Defiance* was regularly employed on traffic in Cornwall and South Devon. This shot in April 1988, which caught the photographer by surprise, shows it working a Tavistock Junction to St Blazey China Clay service near Trematon.

Above:
Coversation piece at Crewe. No 86627
The Industrial Society is to be stabled alongside
Crewe Diesel depot in February 1990. Full
General sector colours, but no Depot Mascot
plate. No 86620 behind it is in its original
Mainline livery.

Below:
For use in the 1991 Railfreight Calendar,
No 60010 *Plynlimon* had General sector decals
applied for a very short period. This rare photo
of it on Kingsferry Bridge, Sittingbourne, has
been copied from the calendar, hence the poor
quality, but it is of historic significance. It is
shown with the permission of EWS and the
Roundel Design Group.

Above:
No 08920 is stabled outside Bescot shed in June 1989. Electrification flashes on roof, and two lamps on front steps. Yellow coupling rods and wasp front end colours. One for the model maker.

Right:
No 37108 takes what should have been empties back to Penmaenmawr over the River Dee Bridge by Chester racecourse in April 1994. Twin headcodes, but no front number or Depot Mascot plate.

Right:
The Wylye Valley line in May 1989, where we see a dirty No 47211 with an Eastleigh to Gloucester Speedlink service at Sherrington. MOD vans from Dinton behind the engine.

Left:
The St Blazey to Cliffe Vale China Clay service is seen here near Eagle Crossing in the West Midlands in June 1989. The locomotive is No 47308. with a non-standard front number and no Depot Mascot plate.

Above:
No 86502 *Lloyd's List* is ready to leave the Freightliner Coatbridge terminal at Gartsherrie with its train to Felixstowe in February 1989. This engine is of interest, since it was one of the very few to receive General sector decals, and is believed to be the only locomotive which carried the Willesden Greyhound Mascot plate, which can be clearly seen here.

Left:
No 86503 *City of Lancaster* is devoid of any embellishments as it brings a rake of empty coaching stock into Euston in May 1989.

Above:
Although the Class 37s and Class 73s were not known to have handled freight services, for the sake of completion of this Sector, examples of each class are shown here. In this view at Tonbridge, No 37609 and No 37604 are seen running light engines from Stewarts Lane to Dollands Moor in August 1995. The glint shows up the three rings and 'eps' flash, which was carried at that time. When used with Eurostar sets, they were normally coupled up with translator flat wagons.

Below:
The first two EPS Class 37s received a black upper bodyside band, which was later replaced by the normal dark grey. A very clean No 37601 was on its way to Dollands Moor in March 1995, when seen here at Sellindge.

Above:
The two EPS Class 73s, No 73118 and No 73130, were fitted with Scharfenberg couplings for moving/rescuing Eurostar sets. The pair are seen here heading into the sun at Kensington Olympia in September 1998. Note that the three rings are on the opposite end of the bodyside, to those of the Class 37s and 92s.

Left:
Ravel is on display at the August 1995 Crewe open day. Note the SNCF identification, the cast nameplate (one of only two such at that time – No 92022 was the other), and the Crewe Electric Depot Mascot plate. White wooden beams for the 3rd rail shoe collectors — they won't stay this clean for long!

Left:
No 92012 *Thomas Hardy* gleams as it takes the first revenue-earning Class 92 hauled train from Wembley to Dollands Moor past Sellindge in July 1996.

Right:
The view is from the multi-story car park by Bromley station, where we see No 92011 *Handel* pass by with the cargo vans from Wembley–Dollands Moor. The date is August 1998, and the mast on the skyline is one of the Crystal Palace TV towers.

Below:
The other Class 92 with a cast nameplate No 92022 *Charles Dickens* is passing Otford Junction in February 1998 with a Wembley to Dollands Moor train of mixed vans. This locomotive is designated for Railfreight Distribution, written out in full, with a mini RFD logo next to it by the cab door. Otherwise a standard EPS Class 92.

LOADHAUL

Above:
Nice and clean No 37517 *St Aidan's C E Memorial School* displays the standard Loadhaul black, orange and yellow scheme at Basford Hall, Crewe open day, but it is missing its front number. August 1995.

Below:
The locomotive contrasts for cleanliness with its train, which is a Departmental working from Grain to Hoo Junction, where it is seen in November 1999. The engine is No 37884 *Gartcosh*.

Right:
No 56045 heads south with a Wilton to Felixstowe Freightliner, as it passes the site of Dringhouses yard, south of York station. A good payload in the evening of an August 1995 day.

Right:
The old 0910 Edinburgh to Reading often required a replacement locomotive by the time it got to Birmingham, often leaving Saltley to find something unusual. This shows the return working to Liverpool, the train having been brought down by Loadhaul No 56035. The date is May 1998, and the spotters at Lower Basildon were very pleased!

Below:
Out of its original territory, No 60059 *Swinden Dalesman* is on the return trip to Margam with the empties from Ebbw Vale. The location is Coedkernew and the date February 1999.

Above:
Stenson Junction in July 1996. No 60025 is in charge of the Kingsbury to Humber empties. This shot, and that previous, show that the orange stripes below the cab windows are not symmetrical. This feature also appeared on some Loadhaul Class 56s, but why it was done this way, heaven only knows.

Below:
Two Loadhaul Class 60s, No 60064 and No 60070, were outshopped i Railfreight two-tone grey with a Loadhaul logo. In this view, No 6007 *James Loudon McAdam* rounds the bend by the gypsy bridge at Wellingborough with Langley to Lindsey empty tanks. March 1997, and no hassle for the photographer!

Left:
This was the sort of train that helped make an interesting picture in September 1997. Mainline blue No 37371 is taking a train of LT 1973 Piccadilly line stock from West Ruislip to Didcot, before heading north to Wakefield for refurbishment. Note the barrier wagons. The location is Manor Farm, Cholsey.

Above:
Another exhibit at the Basford Hall open day in August 1995, this time No 58050 *Toton Traction Depot*. Since the nameplate occupies the far cab side, the Toton Depot Mascot plate has to be placed under the number on the left hand cab side. Single high-intensity headlamp under the nearside lamp cluster. Technical detail label on the nearside cab by the door.

Right:
No 58005 *Ironbridge Power Station* is working hard, pulling the empties from Cottam Power Station up the incline from Retford as it passes Rushey Crossing in July 1996. Standard blue Mainline Class 58, with OHE warning label between cab front windows.

Above:
I have taken many photos at my local station, Winchfield, but never another of a train as overpowered as this Eastleigh departmental to Hoo Junction. The seven wagons are hauled by No 60011, No 37174 in EWS livery, and No 37219 in Mainline blue. The '60' has nothing unusual about it, but there are three OHL warning labels by the roof. The photo was taken in July 1997.

Below:
A more normal shot of the lunchtime Eastleigh to Hoo Junction departmental at Winchfield, this time in October 1996. The two Class 37s show the two versions of Mainline livery, No 37194 *British International Freight Association* in two-tone grey with Mainline decals, and No 37198 in Mainline blue.

Above:
What happens if the doors of a Class 58 get out of order? No 58011 *Worksop Depot* and EWS No 66102 run light engine under Campbell Road Bridge in June 1999.

Right:
No 58041 *Ratcliffe Power Station* has charge of the Calvert to Bristol Binliner as it negotiates Foxhall Junction at Didcot in April 1996. Note the unusual effect of the partially cleaning of the body side.

Right:
The tide is in, the red cliffs glow as No 60009 *Carnedd Dafydd* ambles along the sea wall by Langstone Rock with a Burngullow to Newport ADJ train of China Clay slurry. September 1997.

TRANSRAIL

Below:
Crewe open day in August 1995 showed off two Transrail Class 31s. No 31105 *Bescot TMD* had the large underlined 'T' motif, but no inscription saying 'Transrail' at all. Note the 'Bescot Quality Assured' plate under the nameplate, and the Bescot Depot Mascot Plate. No number on front.

Left:
The other Class 31 was No 31112, in Departmental grey and yellow, with a Transrail 'T' and the word 'Transrail' in white. No Depot Mascot plate. Axle box covers in yellow with red stripe, and white pipe work on only one bogie for some reason — too short of time to finish it?

Below:
Also at Crewe open day was No 37201 *Saint Margaret* in 'Dutch' grey and yellow, with full Trainsrail identification. No front number or Depot Mascot plate and part of the number 3 missing. August 1995.

Right:
No 37906 is seen at Coedkernew with a train of steel bars from Margam to Llanwern in July 1996. Cardiff Canton Depot Mascot Plate and number on nose.

Below:
In April 1996, No 56033 *Shotton Paper Mill* is seen passing through Basingstoke with a Quidhampton to Willesden Calcium Carbonate working. Standard Transrail colours are applied.

Bottom:
The tide is out, but the sun is shining on No 56029 as it crosses the River Usk at Newport, with a Margam to Llanwern MGR train in July 1997.

Left:
Fully finished with all features is Transrail's No 60036 *Sgurr na Ciche* as it speeds past the site of Flax Bourton station in August 1996 with a Burngullow to Irvine China Clay slurry train. The disused siding served a military establishment.

Below:
Away from its normal beaten track, Cardiff's No 60092 *Reginald Munns* ambles north through Radlett station with empties returning from Bow to Croft. The date is July 1997, and the engine caught a glimpse of the sun.

Below:
Before finalising their locomotive colour scheme, Freightliner had one engine painted in a temporary scheme of two-tone green with the red triangular logo. The green shades were not those originally used by BR on the Class 47s. The locomotive concerned was No 47114 named *Freightlinerbulk*, and is seen here in April 2000 at Lower Basildon with a Coatbridge to Southampton Maritime Terminal service. The trees were not throwing shadows on the up main in those days, as they would nowadays.

Right:
Taken prior to the naming ceremony, No 47376 has its nameplate sheeted over, but underneath it says 'Freightliner 1995'. This photo shows the original two-tone grey Freightliner scheme with triangular red logo and the word 'Freightliner' alongside. Unusually, the Crewe Diesel Depot Mascot plate is positioned under the nearside cab window and number. Solid black everywhere under the body, including the buffers.

Below:
A very clean No 47371 rushes a poorly loaded Southampton Maritime to Ripple Lane Freightliner through Winchfield in April 1996.

Below:

A pair of Class 86s, Nos 86606 and 86623, bring a well loaded Freightliner from Leeds to Grain past the suburban station at South Kenton in October 1999. The odd person waits in the shadow for the Bakerloo train approaching in the distance.

Below:

A colour contrast of Freightliner liveries, old and new, are shown on No 86414 *Frank Hornby* in the original two-tone grey with Red flash, and on No 86609 in the current green and yellow livery. The location is Headstone Lane, the date is July 1999, and the train is a Lawley Street to Felixstowe service.

Above:
At a location ruined by platform extensions and extra OHE structures, a pair of Freightliner Class 90s are moving a Felixstowe to Coatbridge train gingerly through the complex layout at Stratford in August 1996. The locomotives are No 90146 and No 90145, which is not only grubby, but has lost all Freightliner identification.

Below:
No 90142 is at full line speed as it passes Carpenders Park in May 1998 with its Crewe to Felixstowe train.

PLAIN GREY

Right:
A very clean No 09024 shows itself off at Redhill in August 1992. For the modeller, note the white lamp brackets and footstep handrails, yellow coupling rods, black underframe and buffers, OHE warning labels by the steps and at roof level, BR double arrow, number and technical data label under the cab, and orange pipework in front of the cab.

Left:
A Pathfinder tour finishing up at Thames Haven is making a long way round to get there, since it is seen here at Bicester Town behind No 31462 in Grey and No 31402 in BR blue, neither being a credit to whoever had prepared them. The date is December 1989. The station looks presentable with the seats painted in Network SouthEast red.

Left:
Bagpipe No 33109 looks quite smart even in plain grey as it stands in Exeter Riverside yard in June 1991. The white lining strips set off the black windows, various bits of pipework are in white, and the Eastleigh Spitfire Depot Mascot plate gleams.

Above:
No 33109 is seen again with a Waterloo to Salisbury semi-fast train near Elvetham. Stock in Network SouthEast colours, and the engine a little duller than at Exeter, but still clean. December 1991.

Right:
Class 37, No 37142 is in charge of a down departmental train at Tiverton Junction in September 1990. The station is out of use, having been replaced by Tiverton Parkway. The footbridge looks somewhat dubious to cross, and the scrap car dealer has plenty of stock for disposal.

Below:
No 37162 and No 37220 bring a diverted Micheldever to Ripple Lane train of tank wagons past Potbridge in November 1992. The lead locomotive has no depot Mascot plate or front number, but has a mini Petroleum sector decal on the body side. The second locomotive is in standard Petroleum sector colours.

Above:
Very clean No 47352 opens up and ruins its carbon footprint as it leaves York station with a Gateshead to Doncaster test train. No front number or Depot Mascot plate. Taken from under Holgate Bridge, when access was possible and legitimate in June 1989.

Left:
First showing of the departmental livery at Bescot open day in May 1990, where No 47333 *Civil Link* is shown with a rake of various wagons in 'Dutch' grey and yellow. No front number, but white wheel rims and pipework on front bogie and yellow axle box covers. Taken early to avoid the crowds!

Left:
No 73108 has certainly been bulled up as it stands in the yard at Eastleigh shed in September 1989. Although it has no Depot Mascot plate, it does have a 73A (Stewarts Lane) shed plate on the front, but it lacks a front number. Even the inside of the horn trumpets have been polished.

'DUTCH' GREY AND YELLOW

Left:
No 26026, with its Eastfield 'Scotty Dog' Mascot plate, shunts wagons at Muirton yard, Perth in March 1991. This was one of the marshalling yards built by British Rail for Speedlink services which never eventuated, and consequently was used merely for departmental purposes. Mainline to Stanley Junction and on to Inverness on the right. What a waste of money.

Right:
No 31107 *John H. Carless V. C.* was on display at the Worksop open day in September 1993. The nameplates are shown in detail on page 10. No front number or Depot Mascot plate.

Below:
A pair of Dutch '31s' head east with a Departmental train near Sandycroft in May 1994. The engines are No 31233 *Severn Valley Railway* and No 31207.

Left:
No 31537 has a Bescot Depot Mascot plate, and a front number on the wrong side. It ambles through Bushey on the down slow with a single wagon northbound Departmental working in June 1993.

Above:
No 31174 takes a train of flats past Kegworth station site in July 1992.

Left:
No 33057 and No 33103 were running round the train they had brought down from Meldon Quarry, when observed in Exeter Riverside yard in September 1990. Note the BR double arrow under the offside cab window on the lead locomotive, and no Depot Mascot plate on either locomotive.

Above:
It is Easter Saturday in April 1992, and there is a shortage of locos, so No 33002 *Sea King* and No 33057 *Seagull* have been commissioned for use on the LSWR main line. The train is an Exeter to Waterloo express and is seen at Newnham.

Below:
Thanks to being tipped off by the signalman at Chard Junction, a shot was obtained of No 37010 hauling an Exeter to Yeovil Junction departmental past Hewish Gates in August 1991. Twin headcodes, but no front number or Depot Mascot plate.

Above:
Steam rises from quenching at Llanwern steelworks, as clean
No 37046 heads West with a breakdown train at East Usk Junction in
February 1991. Although the main line has multiple aspect signals, the
branch is still guarded by a semaphore.

Below:
A loaded train of ballast crosses the main line at Ebbw Junction behind
Class 37 No 37258 in July 1993. Freight is in evidence in ADJ yard,
but motive power has absented itself.

Right:
Ballast is being spread as No 47334 slowly passes though Saunderton station in April 1991. The conductor stands in the cab door keeping an eye on things, and the train is also watched from the platform. The locomotive has a BR double arrow, but no other embellishments.

Above:
No 47975 *Institute of Civil Engineers* is heading west with a gauging train at West Ealing. The lead coach appears to have been converted from a 4TC driving trailer. The month is May, and the year is 1992.

Right:
Forders Siding, Stewartby in May 1995, and No 47366 *Capital Radio's Help a London Child* is ready to leave for Cricklewood with the empty binliner. Signalbox and semaphores are still the order of the day.

Left:
The one and only Class 50 to be painted in Departmental 'Dutch' livery was No 50015 *Valiant* which is seen at Laira in February 1991. Since the '50s' were not re-geared for non-express duties, it seemed a peculiar class to be so treated. Number and BR logo in black.

Left:
'Dutch' liveried, but Transrail logoed No 56049 takes the Quidhampton tanks through Mortimer station in September 1995. This working normally went to Willesden, but on this occasion was diverted to Bescot.

Below:
A busy scene at Tonbridge in July 1993. No 56031 *Merehead* is arriving at the West yard with ballast empties (even though the driver is looking the wrong way!). No 33008 *Eastleigh* and No 33046 *Merlin* wait for business, *Eastleigh* having been restored to original BR green colours, apart from the front number, yellow, panels and high intensity headlamp.

Right:
No 56046 has no identification features whatsoever in this view at Hackney Wick in August 1993. The train is an Ashford to Leyton Departmental.

Above:
Twin '73s' are about to cross the Uckfield branch near Edenbridge with their train of ballast from Godstone Tip to Tonbridge in June 1993. The engines are No 73119 *Kentish Mercury* with Stewarts Lane Depot Mascot plate, and No 73129 *City of Winchester* in Network SouthEast colours.

Right:
No 73131 *County of Surrey* approaches Gatwick Airport with a departmental working for Three Bridges in September 1991. The engine has a Depot Mascot plate, and also a Stewarts Lane 73A shed plate on the front end.

PRIVATE COMPANIES

Right:
Yeoman Class 59 No 59002 brings a loaded stone train from Merehead to Theale past Hungerford Common in May 1986. The town and station of Hungerford are in the background in this view of the English countryside. The locomotive, which has not yet been named, is in original Yeoman colours and in time will become the only one to be painted in Mendip Rail colours. Note how clean the whole train is in these early days of private operations.

Left:
Now repainted into Hanson colours, ARC yellow and grey No 59104 *Village of Great Elm* takes the Allington to Whatley empties through Cuxton station in June 1992. Another complete train of matching locomotive and wagons.

Below:
No 59104 *Village of Great Elm* is seen again taking empties back to Whatley. In this May 1992 shot, it is seen about to pass under the Hayes bypass, when the road was still being built and one could park a car within a coned-off section on the bridge. With OHE all over the place now, this is a shot that cannot be repeated. Southall gasometer dominates the background.

Above:
National Power very kindly gave me permission to take this photo of No 59201 *Vale of York*, which they ran out of the shed specifically for me, so many thanks to them. The location is Ferrybridge, with the power station cooling towers filling the background. The American bell is highly polished to finish off a sparkling locomotive, which is now in EWS red and yellow. October 1994

Below:
The classic scene at Whitley Bridge as National Power No 59205 *Vale of Evesham* leaves Eggborough Power Station with its matched empty hoppers going back for another load of coal. July 1996 is the date.

Left:
Some weedkilling duties were handed over by BR to Hunslet Barclay, who used top-and-tailed Class 20s on these trains. In this view, No 20901 *Nancy*, with No 20904 *Janis* on the other end, is seen at Ascot in August 1992, in the course of a tour round the South Western lines.

Below:
Before privatisation, BR had passed over the handling of nuclear materials to Direct Rail Services. In this view near Churchdown in September 1999, DRS No 37607 and No 20310 are taking a flask from Berkeley to Crewe for onward transit to Sellafield.

Below:
No 20030 and No 20064 are two of three Class 20s painted in green with red solebars, and are seen here at the Basingstoke open day in September 1987. Yellow axle box covers and a full complement of headcode discs.

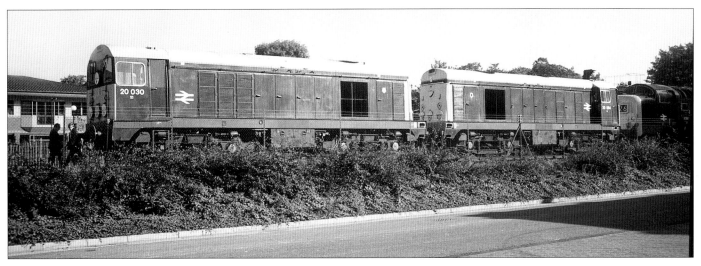

Above:
The Class 37 painted in British Steel blue No 37501 *Teesside Steelmaster* is seen as it heads No 37502 *British Steel Teesside* in Railfreight Red Stripe towards Colton Junction in June 1988. The train is the Corby to Lackenby steel empties.

Right:
No 47145 *Merddyn Emrys* was decked out in a hybrid livery of blue with General sector decals, and an oversize number behind the cab door. The number was carried on the front end, and the Tinsley White Rose Depot Mascot plate shows up well. It is on exhibition at Worksop in September 1993.

Above:
Within a year, No 47145 had its General sector decals replaced by Railfreight Distribution decals, as seen here at Burton Salmon with northbound empty bolsters in November 1994.

Left:
For some reason, one of the locomotives specially painted to celebrate the 150th anniversary of the Great Western Railway was a freight sector engine, rather than a passenger locomotive as were the others. No 47079 *G. J. Churchward* with a GWR crest under the nameplate rests at Westbury in October 1986.

Below:
To celebrate associations with various European railways, three Class 90s were painted in colours of those railways and named accordingly, as was a standard RFD '90'.
The four engines concerned are seen here at a presentation at Trafford Park in October 1993.
No 90022 *Freight Connection* is on the left.
The others are described in more detail opposite.

Right:
No 90128 was painted in SNCB colours and named *Vrachtverbinding.* It had additional yellow below the cab windows to that carried by standard Belgian locomotives, and the Crewe Electric Depot Mascot plate. Of all the three locomotives shown at Rickmansworth in May 1995, this was the most unusual for the Metropolitan line.

Above:
No 90129 *Frachtverbindungen* showed the colours of DB 'White Bib' livery, apart from the mandatory BR yellow end, which rather ruined the effect of the bib. A BR double arrow is seen on the cab side, as this locomotive takes a northbound Freightliner past Headstone Lane in September 1992.

Right:
No 90130 was painted in the colours of a French Class BB26000 Sybic, apart from replacing orange with yellow on the front end. The engine was named *Fretconnection* and was passing Caledonian Road with a freightliner to Felixstowe in October 1992.

Above:
No 37406 *The Saltire Society* is bringing a freight train from Corpach into the yard at Fort William, whence it will form a Speedlink service to Mossend. The locomotive is in original Mainline livery, with the addition of a front number. It is June 1991.

Below:
An unusual choice of locomotive to take the cement empties back from Uddingston to Oxwellmains in May 1986. No 47705 *Lothian* in Scotrail colours approaches Dunbar.

Above:

InterCity No 47676 *Northamptonshire* is given the job of taking a ballast train from Mountsorrel to somewhere in the east of England. It passes Cossington in April 1992.

Below:

Parcels sector No 47569 *The Gloucestershire Regiment* dawdles past South Brent with a departmental working in September 1990. The power to weight ratio should not give any trouble on the South Devon banks.

Above:
Grubby No 47972 *Royal Army Ordnance Corps* in Railway Technical Centre colours has charge of a Southampton Maritime to Coatbridge Freightliner as it passes Silchester in May 1996. Will this train make a profit?

Left:
Superpower for a Dover to St Blazey China Clay empty wagon returning from the continent, passing the site of Doublebois station. It is April 1988, and No 50029 *Renown* is in the original Network SouthEast scheme.

Left:
It is in the evening of a day in April 1985, and No 73127 sparkles in its original Mainline livery as it brings an Eastleigh to Willesden Speedlink service past the up locomotive stabling siding at Woking. A train with a nice variety of wagons.

Right:
Pullman coloured No 73101 *The Royal Alex* has just passed Gatwick Airport station with its Horsham to Redhill departmental train. It is August 1993, but what a comedown for an engine in this scheme!

Right:
One of the two Class 73s painted in Network Blue, No 73004 *The Bluebell Railway* has come off the branch at Fishbourne Junction as it makes its way to Drayton with the stone train from Lavant. Note the special wagons used on this service. May 1989.

Below:
Original Mainline Class 90, No 90036, speeds over the level crossing at Floriston in June 1991 with a Speedlink service from Mossend. Note the height of the wires and the need to stretch the pantograph.

Above:
First sight of an EWS locomotive in July 1996, in this case No 37051 *Merehead* with a ballast train from Mountsorrel at Cossington. The company name is shown as EW&S at that time. The chimney seen in a previous picture has now gone.

Below:
One of the small groups of locomotives painted in EWS colours, No 31466, at the open day at Toton in August 1998. Now lettered EWS with the three heads logo on the right hand cab side.

Above:

Another small group which received EWS colours in the early days of privatisation was the Class 33, of which No 33030 is seen in a similar finish to No 31466, also at Toton. Number on front and appropriate headcode.

Below:

The standard EWS locomotive, Class 66, takes a fully-loaded train of Peugeot cars from Acheres (Paris) to Corby, in the days when there was enough freight traffic through the Channel Tunnel to make a trip to Kent worthwhile. The date is April 1999, the location is Otford Junction and the locomotive is No 66064.

DETAIL AND MISCELLANEOUS PICTURES

Above:
The nameplate of No 58049 *Littleton Colliery*, showing the British Coal logo carried on this series of plates. Standard BR script for the name. Standard red background.

Above right:
No 59003 *Yeoman Highlander* was the Class 59 sent to Germany. The name has a black background, and the EMD works plate shows (in accordance with North American practice) the class as 0-6-6-0. Has this any bearing as to why the JT42CWR is a Class 66, rather than say a Class 62 or 63?

Middle left:
The nameplate of No 37507 has a British Steel logo in addition to its *Hartlepool Pipe Mill* inscription. Black background, and a close-up in full colour of a Thornaby Kingfisher logo.

Middle right:
The Depot Mascot plate for St Blazey is a Cornish Lizard.

Left:
A picture of the cab of No 50149 *Defiance* in General sector colours. Note the rectangular General sector colour strip by the cab door, and the Laira Mayflower Depot Mascot plate